THE LITTLE BOOK

OF

BIG FEARED TRUTHS

"Dr. Demmin writes a thought provoking, easy to follow set of instructions to not only gain greater insight into your Feared Truths, but challenges you to make the necessary changes to improve and enhance your life. I thoroughly enjoyed it!"

—Cindy Coraccio, LCSW

"The bogeyman, which is often projected from within ourselves, is much less horrendous with the lights on. This book turns on the lights . . . for many of my patients it's required reading."

—Dr. Janice Bauer, Ph.D.

"Shakespeare advised, 'To thine own self be true,' but neglected to tell us how. This Little Book does."

—Frances LeMoine, poet

"I find this book working in my life so much. There have been many times lately that I could let what I know isn't true about myself take over. But when it's just me and me, I know the truth and that sustains me."

—Margaret Goddard, veterinary assistant

The Little Book of Big Feared Truths

Overcoming the Main Obstacle to Healthy Self-Esteem

Herbert S. Demmin

Blue Dolphin

Published by Blue Dolphin Publishing, Inc.
P.O. Box 8, Nevada City, CA 95959
Orders: 1-800-643-0765
Web: www.bluedolphinpublishing.com

ISBN: 1-57733-101-X

Library of Congress Cataloging-in-Publication Data

Demmin, Herbert S., 1959–
The little book of big feared truths : overcoming the main obstacle to healthy self-esteem / Herbert S. Demmin.
p. cm.
Includes bibliographical references.
ISBN 1-57733-101-X (pbk. : alk. paper)
1. Self-esteem. I. Title.

BF697.5.S46 D54 2002
158.1—dc21

2002013471

Cover painting, "Leeds Stairway,"
by Elizabeth Solomon, Easthampton, MA

Printed in the United States of America

10 9 8 7 6 5 4 3 2 1

Dedication

To my daughter, Veronica

Contents

Introduction

Feeling awful about yourself is a terrible way to live. Disliking or hating yourself is *the wound* of all wounds. Desperate to feel better, your last defense is to ignore the wound as much as possible. But the pain is still there, and you continue to suffer.

In general, you believe that it's impossible to achieve positive self-esteem if you possess negative self-attributes or beliefs. Perhaps by changing negative personal qualities, you can finally feel good about you. Therefore, you strive to change the qualities you dislike into ones you like. If that doesn't work, you try to convince yourself that your negative self-perceptions and beliefs are wrong. You may even pretend to see yourself more positively. When these strategies fail, you push the negative self-perceptions and beliefs out of awareness, afraid that they make you worthless and rejectable.

Mental health professionals and self-esteem experts often advise people to improve self-esteem by ignoring negative qualities, beliefs, and associated feelings in favor of embracing positive affirmations (Helmstetter, 1986; Brooks & Dalby, 1990). "I'm a good person," "I love me," and "I like myself," are typical examples. Implied in this advice is a belief that persistent, self-berating thoughts are the primary perpetuators of low self-esteem. People are simply in the habit of thinking such thoughts, say the experts. Therefore, we're asked to notice and replace them with self-affirming thoughts. These new thoughts supposedly improve self-esteem. Unfortunately, this "replacement therapy" rarely works because persistent, self-berating thoughts are a *reflection* of low self-esteem, not simply perpetuators of it.

Self-berating thoughts, beliefs, and feelings typically exist because of traumatic or rejecting childhood experiences which convinced us of our inadequacy (Branden, 1972; Bradshaw,

1988). To break the bonds of such beliefs, we need to do more than simply replace the negative with the positive. The memories of these experiences must be explored, and our role in them objectively challenged. Then you can *define yourself*, rather than allow others to do so.

Mental health providers typically believe that negative self-beliefs and associated feelings are overly harsh or inaccurate. They try to convince you of this through salesmanship. This is problematic because they don't allow *you* to explore the evidence regarding your negative qualities. If they embark on such an exploration, they construe the negatives as positively as possible. They do so because they want you to feel better. Moreover, you willingly accept what they say because you want to feel better too. However, if there truly is a basis for feeling bad about yourself, skilled salesmanship about negative self-beliefs and attributes doesn't effect lasting improvements in self-esteem.

The phrase "positive self-esteem" implies that feeling good about yourself precludes harboring negative self-perceptions, beliefs, or feelings. Experts and lay people tend to believe that the path to happiness and fulfillment is to change negative self-perceptions and beliefs into positive ones. In contrast, a "healthy" or "strong" self-esteem reflects self-knowledge and acceptance of positive *and* negative qualities. With healthy self-esteem, one's *self-perception* is not influenced by the feedback of others. The goal of this book is to help you develop a strong self-esteem by embracing all of your decidedly valid personal qualities.

Many books on improving self-esteem are too broad in scope (Branden, 1985, 1987; Bradshaw, 1988). Important points, insights, and strategies for improving self-esteem get lost or diluted by the breadth of their analysis.

Many self-esteem books focus on theoretical and philosophical issues related to the origins, definitions, and significance of low self-esteem, rather than on the task of improving it (Branden, 1971). Those books which emphasize strategies for improving self-esteem are typically complex, and require participation in a many-stepped program which involves the support of both skilled mental health professionals and unskilled lay people (Bradshaw, 1988, 1990).

Other books addressing strategies for improving self-esteem focus on how to heal the "inner child" within (Bishop & Grunte, 1992; Bradshaw, 1990). Such work generally requires the assistance of skilled professionals and participation in the belief of the "inner child" concept, or in childhood patterns of feelings, behaviors, and thinking "inside" of us, which are personified in child form.

Many self-esteem books are inspirational, offer advice regarding happiness and meaning, dos and don'ts, and challenges to self-esteem-damaging beliefs (McGinnis, 1987). Typically, such books are not coherent, organized, and specific in their focus (Newman & Berkowitz, 1971). Many of these books offer the advice to ignore uncorrectable, self-perceived weaknesses, flaws, or regrets (McGinnis, 1987). This contradicts my central hypothesis of learning to accept valid, negative self-perceptions or *Feared Truths*. Lastly, a majority of self-esteem-based books do not offer accounts and dialogue of people struggling with fragile self-esteem and of their attempts to utilize the strategies for improving it which their authors advocate.

In contrast to most books on self-esteem, *The Little Book of Big Feared Truths* is concise, focused, digestible, and easily understood. It is a coherent and organized guide on *strengthening* self-esteem by removing one major obstacle which impedes doing so. As such, its main thesis is not diluted by many self-esteem related issues. It is a "pure" self-help book because its directives can be carried out without the need for skilled mental health professionals and/or large support groups. Lastly, you will find real-life accounts and dialogue of people who have struggled to strengthen their fragile self-esteem interspersed throughout the text.

This book provides an alternative to some of the problematic ways you try to feel better about yourself. It helps you remove one major obstacle to healthy self-esteem: hiding from feared personal qualities. I believe that you can strengthen your self-esteem, and thereby change your life, if you follow the guidelines in the chapters ahead.

1

Feared Truths

One common motivation clients express in therapy is to improve self-esteem. They want to be more confident and to feel better about themselves. With greater self-confidence, they hope to pursue their goals more fervently and successfully with less anxiety or fear.

Many people believe that negative self-perceptions and feelings prevent their happiness and success. I wish I could have better self-esteem. Give me more confidence. Help me feel better about myself. Take away the negative feelings about myself. Convince me I'm not what I fear. This is what we want. This is the road, we think, to improved self-esteem: increase the good feelings and beliefs about myself and decrease the bad.

Unfortunately, improving self-esteem isn't that easy. In fact, most people discover that it is nearly impossible to develop a positive self-esteem by attempting to decrease or get rid of negative beliefs and feelings about themselves. Instead, I have found that helping people create a *healthy* or *strong* self-esteem is the more accessible road to happiness.

Strengthening self-esteem requires the hard work of self-exploration. Remember, fragile self-esteem is typically based on painful, rejecting experiences from childhood, adolescence, and early adulthood. Therefore, detailing a self-esteem-damaging experience can help you glean a different perspective regarding its supposed negative implications about you. However, you may be afraid that your assumed negative role in that experience is true. You don't want evidence of this *Feared Truth*, so you avoid looking at your personally-loaded past.

The fact that we avoid exploring a self-esteem-damaging experience is proof that we fear the validation of some personal inadequacy. This accounts for the *fear* in the phrase "Feared Truths." In addition, such avoidance reflects our vague belief that the inadequacy *will* be validated. If we didn't, we'd be more willing to explore the experience. This accounts for the *truth* in the phrase "Feared Truths."

Thus, a Feared Truth is some quality, action, or inaction of the self which we sense is true but do not want to admit, acknowledge, or believe. We fear its negative implications about our worth and acceptability. As a result, Feared Truths are hidden from ourselves and others.

A closely related concept to Feared Truths is the "shadow." Carl Jung (1950) referred to the shadow as those unwanted and undesirable aspects of ourselves which we disown. We push our shadow aspects out of awareness. Yet, these aspects continue to follow us as surely as our real shadows. In contrast, Jung saw the "persona" as representing those ideal aspects of ourselves which we want to believe and try to present to others. The shadow exists as the opposite of whatever we, as persona, try to present to the world.

A persona is not necessarily a bad or unhealthy way of presenting ourselves. It is a particular role which we have the ability to assume.

The role helps us facilitate successes in specific situations and tasks. You may have a father, husband, comic, tough, athletic, and leadership persona, to name a few.

With our shadows hidden from ourselves and others, our self-image is presented in an acceptable form. But in so doing, we become impostors. In essence, what I have called Feared Truths make up our shadow-self. Thus, we fear the shadow-self; if it's brought to light, we'll be exposed for what we really are. Yet, in our attempts to flee, we're doomed to be forever haunted by it.

One of the most severe consequences of harboring Feared Truths is that you hide them from others too! You're terrified that they will discover your feared-self and throw "evidence" of it in your face. This fear of others can generalize to all situations in your life, resulting in pervasive social anxiety.

Hiding Feared Truths results in social anxiety due to fears of being exposed as an impostor. You worry about Feared Truths being discovered, and hence, of others' potential reactions to you. This results in tremendous self-consciousness. You then construe your anxiety as another negative personal quality. Consequently, your social anxiety is frequently transformed into yet another Feared Truth: you fear others will witness and judge you negatively *because of it.* Isolation, avoidance, and inhibition are utilized to keep this from happening. Yet, these strategies exact a heavy price: you harbor deep regret and discomfort in sensing that you're wasting your life.

Feared Truths cause social anxiety and avoidance, depression, self-consciousness, anger, perfectionism, insecurity, defensiveness, over-sensitivity, and drug addiction. Tragically, these *symptoms* typically become Feared Truths. You fear what others will think of you if they see any of these so-called personality traits. As a result, you *try* to hide these too, increasing the likelihood of further avoidance, inhibition, and lost potential.

There are many ways to protect oneself from exposing Feared Truths to others. Jeff, for instance, experienced a "breakdown" in high school. As a result, he feared being seen as inadequate and crazy. This fear expressed itself in many ways. For example, he lied about living with his parents, why he wasn't in college, and why he drove a delivery truck for a living. He couldn't tolerate the idea of anyone looking down on him. He lied or said something clever and comical in response to those who happened to mention any one of these realities. Eventually, he decided to stop dating and going to work, fearing rejection and failure because of negative implications about his self-worth. Soon, the idea of dying seemed safer than that of living.

Alan feared anyone who might verify his unacceptable belief that he was ugly. He occasionally acknowledged this fear to me, but did so in a consistently harsh fashion. He was unable to inspect this belief long enough to thoroughly evaluate it. He was terrified of what he might confirm. In addition, he hid this Feared Truth from others by isolating at home and avoiding social encounters as much as possible.

Gary had learning disabilities as a child. He feared that he was stupid. He memorized poems and word lists to convince people otherwise, or at least to keep them "off the scent." At a greater extreme, he didn't miss a day of work in thirty years, no matter how sick or injured he was. His Feared Truth of being dumb made him feel dispensable. Therefore, if he was never absent from work, he thought, he could never be replaced. In addition, his reliability was a compensation for feeling undeserving of the job, given his Feared Truth. Not surprisingly, Gary felt *extremely* anxious all day and every day.

All three of these individuals were chronically anxious. They were anxious when alone, as they anticipated social encounters, and of course, during them as well. In addition, the consequences of their "protective" strategies left them depressed, and even suicidal.

Despite the suffering caused by our protective strategies, it's a price most of us are willing to pay. Having been hurt on many occasions, especially throughout childhood and adolescence, we feel as if we can't tolerate more wounds. We fear we're inadequate, unlovable, and worthless, either generally or in many specific ways. It hurts so much to feel stupid, ugly, fat, or unpopular, that we fear further evidence which might support such self-perceptions. As a result, we continue to utilize our destructive, "protective" strategies.

When yet another experience occurs which reinforces some negative concern about ourselves, it really hurts, but doubly so because it's a reminder of prior wounds. Our pain and shame are intensified because past, pain-laden memories resurface in the present. We typically don't recognize that our pain is a reflection of this past pain as well. Instead, we experience it as the pain of the present, and as further "proof" of our inadequacy. It's huge, intense, and overwhelming. We can't tolerate it. It's too much. We must escape it at all costs. There's little else so hurtful as feeling horrible about ourselves.

And yet, there's really no escape through these strategies to protect ourselves from Feared Truths. The strategies are too inhibiting and actually reinforce our negative self-perceptions and feelings.

2

The Origins of Feared Truths

Drawing on the work of many theorists and researchers, Ken Wilber (1996) outlines the form a child's sense of self takes as he develops. As a toddler, a child's sense of self is rooted in his body. As he gets older, his sense of self becomes tied to verbal dialogue. This dialogue takes the form of thoughts and speech.

Around the age of seven, the child's internal dialogue includes his parents' beliefs, demands, prohibitions, and so on. In addition, his parents' attitudes, feelings, and beliefs *about him* are reflected in his thoughts. In other words, the quality of the relationship between the child and his parents becomes thought-bound. Taking the form of thoughts, an internal dialogue of roles begins, where the child "plays the parts" of his parents and himself, interacting. He can take the role of parent toward himself. The child may, for example, scold himself for being selfish, resulting in feelings of guilt, or praise himself for finishing his chores, resulting in feelings of pride. His sense of self, bound to his thoughts, becomes differentiated into roles based on his original relationships. These role-voices also become associated with particular images, feelings, and memories.

Let's elaborate on those thought-bound roles in which we get consumed. Eric Berne (1974) is credited with the important concept of "scripts." As a child's developing sense of self settles in his thoughts and away from his body, he is subject to being "programmed" or "brainwashed." In other words, says Wilber (1996), the parents have the power to insinuate themselves "into the significant roles of the child's internal dialogues." To the extent that a child's sense of self is bound to what he thinks, he will be programmed by the internalized, voiced-roles of significant others. He will be assigned a script in response to these "voices," much as an actor is to a scripted role. If these internalized voices are messages of unacceptable inadequacy, he will have grave self-doubts and a fragile self-esteem.

Under the influence of these "voiced" roles, certain qualities of the self are selectively screened out of awareness due to parental prohibitions, for example. Some of these suppressed qualities are Feared Truths and make up one's shadow.

Thus, as thought-selves, we are subject to viewing ourselves according to how others have treated us. This leaves us inherently vulnerable to the feedback of people, especially as children.

Wilber (1996) indicates that children seven years and older have a need to fit in and belong. This need leaves them vulnerable because they are "other-focused." They are concerned about fitting in and focus on others to figure out how to manage it. Furthermore, the inexperience of children requires that they learn from others the social roles and rules of various interpersonal situations. They need to learn their roles in relation to those of others at home, school, church, and the neighborhood. For the most part, their roles are determined by how others see, react to, and treat them. They learn about themselves through the feedback of others. In this regard, the people in their lives are like mirrors. Through others, a given child may see himself as the class clown, good athlete, ugly geek, shy kid, or stupid son. Moreover, convinced of these self-identities, he acts accordingly, unable to imagine he could be any different.

Children are also vulnerable to seeing themselves through others because they can't self-observe: they're consumed in *being* their actions, experiences, thoughts, and beliefs. However, during early adolescence, children begin to objectify and reflect on their thoughts, beliefs, and experiences. As a result, they can judge, question, or challenge what they've been led to believe about themselves and the world. Unfortunately, their protective strategies from Feared Truths can be so entrenched, they don't utilize this ability to self-observe and evaluate their emotionally-laden, "other-colored" self-perceptions and beliefs. Indeed, they continue to be totally other-focused and other-concerned.

For instance, thirty year old Lauren said that throughout her childhood she was told what to do. She cleaned the house, cooked, did laundry, and looked after her brothers and sisters. Her entire childhood was determined for her. It was dictated that she function as a child-servant. She came to realize that her needs, feelings, and opinions were insignificant. Consequently, she felt insignificant and worthless.

Lauren came to therapy due to a drunk driving arrest. She said that she was an alcoholic. Within the first few weeks of seeing her, she had two "slips." She went out with friends one night and had eight or nine drinks. She said that the worst part of this was how awful she felt about herself the next day, breaking her sobriety once again.

I asked Lauren what made her think that she was an alcoholic. Perplexed, she said things like, "I just can't drink," "Everybody always told me I was," "Every therapist I ever had said I was," and "My mom said I was going to be just like my Dad." When I asked for evidence of her alcohol problem, she became more baffled. All that stumbled out was, "That's what people have always told me."

Over time, Lauren recalled "fall-out" from actual drinking experiences. She experienced occasional hangovers at work the next day, along with the recent drunk driving charge. She could think of no other problematic outcomes from her drinking. I asked her about other possibilities, such as withdrawal symptoms, signs of tolerance, social problems, vocational lapses, and family difficulties, but she earnestly denied them all. Subsequently, when I asked if she was an alcoholic, she couldn't answer. She wasn't accustomed to forming her own opinions about this or anything else. She left in a very pensive state, saying she had to let all of this sink in.

Lauren said that during periods when her intent was to stay sober, her "slips" went overboard because, having "blown it" already, she might as well "go all the way." This convinced her that she was indeed an alcoholic, but now she wondered if this potentially false view of herself caused her to drink too much when she did "slip." Lauren decided that she'd use future drinking experiences to evaluate whether or not she is a problem drinker. This time, however, she will make a decision about herself, forming her own opinions.

Lauren's issues, in part, reflect her long-standing dependency on others to decide what she should be, do, feel, believe, like and dislike. This tendency had its origins in childhood, when she was vulnerable to the dictates of others. Consequently, she didn't know herself. It seems no surprise that she was indecisive about almost every issue in her life. When Lauren started to define herself, she began to change in positive ways.

You, like many of us, continue to allow others to define your worth, adequacy, and personal qualities. It's an unnecessary and unhealthy holdover from your past. You can escape this trap if you become the authority on your self-identity. As the final authority on who you are, others' reactions to you are always considered in the light of your own. Think about it. How frequently do you depend on feedback as a way to judge yourself in a situation? You're so vulnerable as a result. In essence, your self-esteem lies in the hands of others! You're giving people too much power, your power!

3

Identifying Feared Truths

Twenty-five years ago, while Todd was hitchhiking with two of his nineteen year old friends, he was attacked by two huge men, one wielding a machete and the other, a crowbar. By the time he saw them out of the corner of his eye, it was too late; he was hit over the eyebrow and knocked to one knee. He felt terrified, and ran away as fast as he could.

Throughout high school, Todd had a reputation as a tough, "fearless," easygoing kid, who everybody liked and respected. He was on the wrestling team and won two fights against bigger foes. He remembered that he hadn't a care in the world during high school.

Unfortunately, Todd's life changed dramatically after the hitchhiking incident. He was suddenly filled with fear. He was terrified of getting into another fight. He was particularly afraid while driving: he wouldn't look another driver in the eye for fear of starting a confrontation. As an adult, he became agoraphobic, rarely leaving his home unless he had to. In addition, throughout his long-term employment at two jobs, he felt less competent than his co-workers and was pervasively anxious about being exposed as an impostor.

Despite his fears, no one else knew about them. Todd pretended to be that tough, carefree, easy-going person that he had been in high school. At work, he pretended to be as competent as everyone else. This strategy of pretense exacted a heavy price: Todd was horribly anxious and became seriously depressed about his limitations and lost opportunities. In therapy, he identified his major Feared Truth of being a coward, given his terror during the hitchhiking attack. He was ashamed of the fear he felt during that attack and of the fact that he ran away. Such fear was inconsistent with his self-image and with the reputation he had earned in high school.

As an adult capable of defining yourself, stop pretending your Feared Truths don't exist. Stop hiding them from yourself and others. Learn to deal with them in a new way. This starts with the process of discovering and identifying your Feared Truths.

This process begins by listing your negative qualities. Some of these qualities may turn out to be Feared Truths. Therefore, listing your negative qualities may be extremely difficult. It can be painful and frightening to get close to these potential Feared Truths. Consequently, you may have difficulty owning any negative qualities.

Below, eleven strategies are discussed to help you generate a list of negative qualities. Among these, you should be able to identify Feared Truths, if you have any.

FINISH INCOMPLETE SENTENCES

Nathaniel Branden (1985, 1987) has written many helpful books on self-esteem. He asks his readers to finish a list of incomplete sentences to identify their negative qualities (Branden, 1987). This is an extremely useful task which prompts potential Feared Truths in a spontaneous and experientially vivid fashion. Dr. Branden recommends that we complete each sentence stem with 6-10 different endings. He asks us not to worry about the literal truth of each ending. He says that we need not concern ourselves if one ending conflicts with another. He recommends that we finish the sentences without criticism or censorship. In other words, be spontaneous.

Listed below are Branden's (1987) sentence stems. I recommend that you do not read any further until completing these stems.

I like myself least when I—

It's not easy for me to admit that—

It's not easy for me to be self-accepting when I—

Sometimes I dislike myself when I—

One of the things I dislike about myself is—

Mother gave me a view of myself as—

Father gave me a view of myself as—

If I were willing to look fully at what I did (or failed to do)—

The hard thing about being honest with myself is—

The hard thing about being honest with others about myself is—

One of the emotions I have trouble accepting is—

One of the thoughts I tend to push out of my mind is—

One of the things about my body I have trouble accepting is—

Look at your responses to these incomplete sentences. They should clearly reflect negative qualities that you believe or fear you have. You should recognize them as consistent with your history of self-concerns. Write down these negative qualities as part of your list of potential Feared Truths.

CONSIDER COMMON FEARED TRUTHS

Add to this list of potential Feared Truths by asking yourself if you have concerns, fears, or negative beliefs about your appearance and intelligence, the two most common Feared Truths with which people seem to struggle. Consider other common Feared Truths such as poverty (which is usually equated with inadequacy and failure), non-masculinity/femininity, unpopularity, lack of sexual prowess, non-athleticism, and alcohol/drug problems (which are commonly associated with weakness, selfishness, and irresponsibility, to name a few). You should recognize the personal applicability of some of these common Feared Truths almost immediately. Most of us are all too aware of long-standing concerns about ourselves.

CONSIDER HURTFUL COMMENTS ABOUT YOU AFTER A PARTY

You can get in touch with Feared Truths by imagining being at a party where you meet many new people. When you leave, imagine eavesdropping on what they say about you. What would hurt or bother you the most? Close your eyes and imagine this. List what comes to mind.

Jason was having trouble identifying potential Feared Truths. In fact, despite fears of socializing, asking women out on dates, and certain failure experiences, he insisted that he didn't have low self-esteem. After overhearing an imagined conversation fellow party-goers were having about him, he said that he was afraid they would think of him as a "loser." They would talk about him being a high-school dropout, "... of not taking anything to the next level, except for restaurant management, which is too basic and easy," and of being "good for nothing." He said that these reactions would mean that he was a loser. "Hearing them say things about me, not to my face, would hurt me even more," he said. This basic exercise helped Jason identify one of his Feared Truths.

CONSIDER QUALITIES YOU DISLIKED ABOUT YOURSELF IN THE PAST

You can discover Feared Truths by *recalling* what you disliked about yourself as a child or adolescent. Were you preoccupied with concerns about your crooked teeth, old clothing, reading problems, or weight? List the negative qualities that you recall disliking, hating, or of which you felt ashamed.

CONSIDER QUALITIES OTHERS DISLIKED ABOUT YOU

What you disliked about yourself in the past typically reflected what others disliked about you, as well. Therefore, it helps if you recall the negative things others said to or about you that really hurt. How did schoolmates react to you? How did teachers, parents, friends, and strangers treat you? List the negative qualities that come to mind.

CONSIDER THE NEGATIVE QUALITIES OF YOUR PARENTS AND SIBLINGS

Another area worth exploring when considering Feared Truths are the negative qualities your parents and siblings had or have. You may have feared that you would turn out like mom or dad in certain ways. Perhaps you thought this was your genetic destiny. Dad was an alcoholic, a liar, violent, lazy, uneducated, prejudiced, and narrow-minded. Mom was anoretic, overly strict, a workaholic, and depressed. As a child you may have disliked, been ashamed of, felt embarrassed by, or even hated certain qualities your parents possessed. You may have decided to *never* be like that. You couldn't stand yourself if you turned out like them. Therefore, you suppress such qualities and project their opposites.

Siblings often try to establish a unique role for themselves in their family; they try to be very different from their brothers and sisters. They may be extra-motivated to be different from their siblings due to certain qualities, behaviors, or tendencies their parents reject in them. In addition, they frequently decide that they hate some things about their brothers and sisters, and won't tolerate it in themselves. For example, you despised your sister's sloppiness, and knowing your mom was just as disgusted with her, you become a "neat freak." Over time, you discover that you can't stand the least bit of untidiness, feeling compelled to clean, even when you'd prefer doing something else. You also hated your brother's sickliness. Therefore, as an adult, you have difficulty expressing your needs and vulnerabilities. Similarly, you don't reach out to others for help. Lastly, your other brother had learning problems, of which your father seemed ashamed. As a result, you develop strong study habits and begin to experience extreme test anxiety in college.

Ask yourself what you didn't and don't like about your mother, father, brothers, and sisters. Write down those qualities and decide which ones you dislike the most or toward which you have the strongest negative feelings. Ask yourself if you share any of these qualities. Notice any difficulty you may have in acknowledging their existence. Notice your emotional reactions as you consider the personal, historical evidence which suggests that you may share the quality under consideration. If you have strong emotions and/or adamantly deny the presence of this quality, past or present, you may be close to a Feared Truth.

CONSIDER THE POSITIVE QUALITIES OF YOUR PARENTS AND SIBLINGS

Sometimes we feel as if we could never live up to our parents' or siblings' good qualities. Dad frequently mentioned being a genius, belonged to a smart people's group called "Mensa," and was president of his company. He berated people with less money and education than he. His daughter became afraid of not living up to his standards, and believed she could never be as smart.

Jenny's mom was prom queen in high school and later earned second place in the state's beauty contest. Her mom was fussy about her appearance and seemed overly concerned about Jenny's. Deep down, Jenny believed she could never be as beautiful as her mom, which truly meant she was inadequate.

Thus, you can further explore your potential Feared Truths by considering your parents' positive qualities. What were they? How did they leave you feeling about yourself? Did you become afraid that you didn't share their strengths? Was it a problem if you didn't? List what comes to mind.

CONSIDER THE OPPOSITES OF YOUR DRIVES, MOTIVATIONS, AND GOALS

The psychologist Alfred Adler (1929) believed that much of one's personality, characteristic drives, motives, aspirations, actions, and feelings, to name a few, could be accounted for by that which one feels inferior. He coined the term "inferiority complex" for individuals who are driven to make strides away from the qualities about which they feel inadequate.

Therefore, you can discern potential Feared Truths by assessing your major motivations, drives, and goals. Once you name them, look at and list their opposites as a way to discover a potential Feared Truth. One client engaging in this process looked at the fact that he only read nonfiction. In fact, he was driven to do so. He was trying to ensure that he was always learning something. The opposite of learning is not-learning. He realized that this motive to learn was tied to a Feared Truth that he was dumb.

CONSIDER YOUR NEGATIVE REACTIONS TO OTHERS

You can discover potential Feared Truths by paying attention to your strongest negative reactions to people. For example, homophobia, having strong, negative reactions about homosexuality, often reflects the presence of Feared Truths. I have had several male clients who were sexually abused by men as children. As a result, they grew up fearing they were "gay," often due to unexplored beliefs that they played some willing role in what happened. As adults, they seemed to fear the possibility of "gay" men "coming on" to them. They feared that something "gay" about their presentation may have prompted this "come on," thereby suggesting evidence of a willing role in their prior molestation.

Larry said a co-worker recently made a "joking," sarcastic comment in front of others about not checking some specification sheets, which resulted in a mistake. Larry was furious and nearly got into a fist fight with this man. As it happened, he screamed and swore at him, creating a huge scene. Larry and I recognized that his co-worker activated the Feared Truth that he was dumb, and hence, an engineering impostor.

There are many "every day" examples of people having strong, negative reactions to others. Having intense, negative reactions to someone's anger, self-centeredness, alcoholic drinking, wealth, lying, stealing, prettiness, efficiency, popularity, fat, slenderness, and so on, can reflect underlying Feared Truths about yourself. Ask yourself, "Why did I have such a strong reaction to him?" "Could it be I'm afraid I have the same negative quality?" "Could it be that I fear I don't have the same positive quality?" List those qualities towards which you have strong, negative reactions.

CONSIDER YOUR NEGATIVE REACTIONS TOWARD YOURSELF

Your harsh, negative thoughts toward yourself can reflect potential Feared Truths. About what are you hardest on yourself? List those qualities and tendencies about which you are your worst critic.

For instance, Mitch was constantly berating himself about the quality of his car, how low his hourly work wage was, and living at home with his parents. Mitch came to understand that these harsh thoughts about himself reflected his Feared Truth of being a "loser." Mitch's father had been an alcoholic, didn't work, was a "couch potato," and often told him that he was a loser too.

CONSIDER YOUR REGRETTED ACTIONS OR INACTIONS

It's common for people to fear certain negative personal qualities based on regretted actions or actions not taken. They often end up making some stigmatizing generalization about themselves, as a result. Typically, the generalization and the regretted experience associated with it are pushed out of awareness as much as possible. For example, when Hank was twelve years old, a classmate, Kevin, tried to start a fight with him. When Kevin rushed him, his classmates intervened and prevented the confrontation. Hank remembered being really scared of fighting Kevin. However, he pretended to be held back by the other boys. He recalled that one of them said, "Hank's scared, he really doesn't want to fight." Hank knew this was true. He became afraid that he was a coward. From that point on, he avoided fist fights at all costs and worried about any situation which might present the possibility of a fight. He was afraid of being exposed to himself and others as a coward.

Thus, to complete your list of potential Feared Truths, consider experiences consisting of regretted actions or actions not taken. Give yourself time to recall such experiences. You will likely resist this task; little will come to mind. In time, however, when you remember significant events, write them down. Be honest with yourself about the regretted action or inaction. Identify the qualities that you feared the action or inaction reflected in you. Include these qualities on your list of potential Feared Truths.

In this chapter, I asked you to muster the courage to identify and list your negative qualities, and hence, potential Feared Truths. To assist you, I asked you to engage in a number of tasks:

Finish incomplete sentences
Consider common Feared Truths
Consider hurtful comments about you after a party
Consider qualities others disliked about you
Consider qualities you disliked about yourself
Consider negative qualities of parents and siblings
Consider positive qualities of parents and siblings
Consider the opposites of your drives, motivations, and goals
Consider your negative reactions to others
Consider your negative reactions toward yourself

Consider your regretted actions and inactions

Your active participation in generating a list of negative qualities and potential Feared Truths is the difficult but necessary first step to strengthening your self-esteem. Having done so, scan this list and rank-order the negative qualities. In other words, put the quality which you most fear is true at the top of the list. Then pick out the number two negative quality, the number three, and so on. The negative qualities at the top part of your list are your likely Feared Truths. Now you are ready for the next step of finally becoming the authority on who you are.

4

Giving Yourself a Fair Hearing

Hiding Feared Truths is a game of shame, fear, pretense, and desperation. You want the game to end, but you can't stop playing. You're ashamed of negative personal qualities, and are convinced that they make you worthless and rejectable. You fear their truth and discovery. You desperately long for others to disconfirm your feared-self. As a result, your self-esteem is in their hands. Therefore, everyone becomes frightening and dangerous in their potential to damage your self-worth.

Your self-esteem is largely determined by how others treated you as a child, adolescent, and young adult. Consequently, as an adult, it is imperative that you reevaluate your "other-colored" Feared Truths. Having your list of Feared Truths in front of you, can you objectively evaluate their validity?

It's amazing how many people have never explored the validity of their supposed negative qualities. They've been scared of discovering that these qualities are absolutely true. Consequently, they harbor vague, intense fears about themselves without ever challenging or exploring what they've been led to believe.

Paradoxically, we hope that others will disconfirm Feared Truths that we hide from ourselves and them. The disconfirmation we seek comes in the form of certain positive reactions, the opposite of which we fear are true. For instance, Mary is determined to be nice and never get angry. She lives for others to tell her how sweet she is. John is preoccupied with being "macho." He's proud when men seem intimidated by him. Jacob is driven to make one hundred thousand dollars a year. He's thrilled when women are impressed by his car. By depending on others to disconfirm Feared Truths, our self-esteem is in their hands.

I'm concerned when I hear a client relish positive feedback that someone gave her, especially when I know she is anxious and sensitive about negative feedback. I frequently remind her, "Live by the sword, die by the sword." In other words, if positive feedback significantly influences her feelings about herself, it's likely that negative feedback will too.

To steal back your self-esteem, you must be your own judge by putting Feared Truths on trial during a *Fair Hearing*. At a Fair Hearing, you decide, once and for all, what to include and exclude as parts of your self-identity. Subsequently, you will stop depending on others to disconfirm Feared Truths, and you'll be less afraid of and vulnerable to them.

To give yourself a Fair Hearing, recall the experiences related to the Feared Truth from the vantage point you had at that time. Try to remember what happened and what it was like to go through the experiences connected to the Feared Truth, as you lived them. Try to remember what you felt and thought at the time. Recall how you understood the experiences at that time. Recall your general circumstances, where you lived, who was in your life, your varied stresses, your support, and what your day-to-day life was like. In general, try to remember what it was like to be you going through those experiences.

As you recall the details from your subjective past, write down what you remember. Narrate your story in the first person, using "I-statements" throughout. For example, "Living my life then, I felt a daily loneliness. Dad was gone and mom always worked. There was little attention or affection to go around; there were so many of us kids. When George, my little league baseball coach came along, he gave me tons of attention. I ate it up. He gave me so many things: money, gifts, and he took me to some great places. We went to Red Sox games, arcades, and he took me to his work. But when I didn't do what he wanted, he took it all away. His angry silence made me feel so bad and guilty. I couldn't stand it. I had to give in."

Reevaluate the Feared Truth "on trial" as you recall the details of your past. But be sure to avoid the following pitfalls as you recall the events related to your Feared Truths.

Avoid allowing the judgments of others, and the emotional pain associated with each Feared Truth, to contaminate *your* reevaluation.

Upon recalling painful memories, you re-experience some of that pain. This pain can reconfirm your belief in some negative attribute or Feared Truth. For example, Stanley recalled the pain and shame he felt while being teased by kids about his teeth. Those feelings seemed to embody the fact that he was ugly. As he felt them again, they biased his present self-judgments regarding his appearance.

With emotionally-laden, Feared Truth-based experiences, do your best to set aside your feelings, at least temporarily, and objectively evaluate those experiences as thoroughly as possible. In addition, try to ignore what others have told you about each Feared Truth, and decide, between you and you, which one is true or has merit, and which does not. This is no easy task, but it is necessary nonetheless.

Avoid vague, biased, retrospective views about the Feared Truth-based experiences

Another pitfall to avoid during a Fair Hearing is the tendency to embrace vague, biased, retrospective views about the past which are unfair and inaccurate. This is one of the most problematic tendencies adults have: they prejudge the past through the eyes of the present.

There is a wide chasm between how we experience the world now versus how we experienced it as children. Intellectually, we know that children experience their world differently than adults. But we often lose sight of this fact when judging our childhood selves. I frequently hear adult clients say, "I should have known better," "I should have done something about it," "I must have deserved what happened," "I was a wimp," to name a few. How swiftly these prejudgments pass once we allow ourselves to recall the past through childhood eyes. Clients almost always realize, "How I behaved at that time made sense given what was happening and how I understood it then."

Avoid the "Hindsight is 20-20" trap

The cliche, "Hindsight is 20-20," is often at work when we are overly critical of our childhood selves. We literally forget, as we so zealously look at things from our more informed, adult vantage point, that we were less informed then as children. We forget that, as children, we didn't know how to behave in a more adaptive fashion because we didn't know how things would turn out. We also forget that we lacked the emotional, intellectual, and practical resources that our adult selves possess.

Anthropomorphism is the tendency to ascribe human qualities to animals. I believe that there is a similar tendency to ascribe adult abilities, ways of thinking, and understanding, to children. We're so absorbed in our adult vantage points, we can't begin to relate to our childhood selves.

In sum, to give yourself a Fair Hearing you must "admit" all of the evidence relevant to the Feared Truth "on trial." This is historical, experiential evidence potentially confirming or disconfirming the validity of the Feared Truth. Take a close look at this evidence. Don't let feedback and reactions from the past influence your judgments regarding the potential validity of the Feared Truth. Set aside the associated feelings, and objectively evaluate the Feared Truth-based experiences as best you can. Judge for yourself what appears to be valid evidence confirming or disconfirming the Feared Truth. Remember what you went through and what it was like to be you during that experience. Try to avoid vague, biased, retrospective prejudgments about the experiential evidence. Avoid the "Hindsight is 20-20" trap. Put yourself "in the shoes" of your past self. Try to avoid judging your child-self, if applicable, through adult eyes.

These subjectively-based recollections form the basis of your Fair Hearing. Once all of this personal, historical evidence is on paper, study it. Your task is to decide whether or not the evidence supports your Feared Truth. On a piece of paper, list the evidence supporting and not supporting the Feared Truth in separate columns. Be your own judge, jury, prosecuting, and defense attorney. Take these roles out of the hands of past and present others. If you think there is substantial evidence to support your Feared Truth, accept the factual basis for it: "Yes, I am this way" or "Yes, I have been this way."

Larry worked as an engineer and feared he was dumb. This Feared Truth stemmed from grade school academic struggles, coupled with the feedback of disappointed adults. Consequently, Larry felt like an impostor and feared being exposed as dumb to his supervisors, colleagues, friends, and family.

Weighing the evidence of Larry's Feared Truth, he recalled that in his grade school classrooms his mind wandered. He remembered being preoccupied by thoughts and fantasies, especially when the subject matter was boring and tedious. As a result, his grades suffered. Importantly, he was able to concentrate when the subject matter was interesting. Similarly, in his work as an engineer, Larry says that his mind wanders when the task at hand is boring, tedious, or mundane. He often makes mistakes as a result.

This straightforward recollection helped Larry better specify the nature of his difficulty. Perhaps he wasn't dumb after all? Perhaps he had an attention problem, one that expressed itself during boring tasks. Larry decided that this perspective was more accurate and specific than his prior one. He also decided that his attention problem was still a "deficiency" and something he didn't feel good about. Nevertheless, he became less afraid of and more able to accept it as a personal limitation.

Alan was born with a physical condition affecting his appearance. He was six feet, five inches tall, slender, had big hands, big feet, and long limbs. His face was extremely long and thin. He had a large nose, dark circles under his eyes, a long chin, and strong overbite. He had an extremely difficult childhood and painful adolescence. His parents were ashamed of his appearance. As an adult, he continued to have many humiliating and crushing experiences at the hands of cruel people who criticized and rejected him. Such rejections included being called "horse face" by fellow college students in his dorm. Consequently, he came to see himself as a tall, foreboding "monster." He felt compelled to "protect" *others* from having to look at him by isolating in his room.

During the first part of therapy Alan could not bear to discuss his appearance. Instead, he shared other aspects of his painful past. Eventually, he courageously discussed his physical self-perception. I urged him to begin assessing his appearance as objectively as possible.

Initially, Alan said it was impossible to separate the horrible wounds of the past from his struggle to objectively evaluate the validity of his Feared Truth. In time, however, he was able to verbalize a more objective description of his appearance. He decided that he was "unattractive" and "ugly," but had nice hair and liked certain features of his body. This was both a big and small step for Alan. He continued to feel awful about his appearance, but these feelings became less intense and harsh. You might not see this change in his self-perception as very dramatic, but I believe it brought positive changes in his life and represented a good start. For one, he became less concerned about others' potential reactions to him. He was still scared of people, but began to socialize a little bit more.

Given one's long-standing and habitual mind-set associated with Feared Truths, this Fair Hearing process needs to be intermittently repeated. The best time to revisit a Fair Hearing is when you're absorbed in some of the problematic reactions likely stemming from Feared Truths. Such reactions might include intense, negative reactions to others, harsh, negative reactions toward yourself, or avoidance of situations.

When you notice and identify the Feared Truth lurking behind a problematic reaction, remind yourself of the evidence "admitted" during its Fair Hearing. What was your prior decision regarding the Feared Truth given this evidence? If the evidence was primarily disconfirming, enjoy the relief experienced in your more accepting attitude toward it and yourself. If the evidence was confirming, be willing to embrace the Feared Truth and its associated feelings, rather than engaging in escapist reactions.

5

After Your Fair Hearing

How do you know when you have truly accepted a Feared Truth? The most telling proof is your ability to openly acknowledge it. We all agree that you can't share everything about yourself, indiscriminately. That's just silly and beyond common sense. But you should be able to share a Feared Truth with a trusted person, at the very least.

Many of us will only open up to people we trust, meaning those who won't judge, hurt, or criticize us. This, however, is often a sign of our continued vulnerability to and fear of critical reactions, and suggests that we haven't accepted valid Feared Truths, along with their painful aspects. Therefore, the ultimate proof of having accepted Feared Truths is your ability to deal with anyone who knows about them, no matter what their reactions.

Your feelings about yourself won't be as affected by negative feedback when you become the authority on your personal qualities, both positive and negative. When this is the case, no one can tell you anything you don't already know about yourself. In addition, if you can feel the emotions associated with any decidedly valid Feared Truth, then others' comments will affect you much less. They're not triggering emotions that you haven't been willing to feel. Can they make you feel worse about this self-perceived, valid Feared Truth than you already do? In my opinion, the answer to this question is "no." Even if they push their harsh judgments too far, you'll recognize that they surpass your own.

Let me give an example. For a long time, Larry wanted an earring but feared that others would see him as foolish. They would think that he was trying to be youthful in a way that was silly and beyond his years. In addition, he anticipated that people might think of him as "gay."

Yet, he wouldn't be bothered by the latter because, "I know I'm not." While exploring this he realized that *he believed* having an earring was silly and beyond his years. That's why he would be bothered by similar feedback from others. Part of him felt this way already but he couldn't entirely accept it. He hid it from himself and therefore needed to hide it from others.

Some people may criticize what you deem a valid, Feared Truth. Because your Fair Hearing has resulted in feelings of confidence that you're the authority on your self-identity, you could openly agree with their criticism. I find that people often respect your ability to be so honest and courageously self-informed.

When you accept a decidedly valid Feared Truth, you become much less concerned about and vulnerable to others' opinions of you. This lesser vulnerability to others is extremely empowering! Your self-esteem no longer lies in their hands. No one frightens you. Nothing left to hide. Nothing left to be discovered. No longer an impostor to yourself or anyone else. What a relief! What freedom!

Another typical outcome of accepting your decidedly "valid" Feared Truths is that you're in a better position to change them. Of course, some Feared Truths can't be changed, but others certainly can. Generally, you're too busy running and hiding from Feared Truths to do anything about them. You can't change them unless they're acknowledged, and they can't be acknowledged unless you're willing to experience the feelings associated with them.

I'm often asked, "How long does it take to accept Feared Truths?" The answer to this question depends on you. You may never accept a Feared Truth or you could accept one instantly. Owning a Feared Truth requires a shift in attitude about it. Once you understand what your Feared Truth is, how you've been hiding from it, and how much suffering your hiding has caused, you often experience an attitude shift. You recognize that it will be a relief to finally explore and give yourself a Fair Hearing about the Feared Truth, rather than allow it to run your life.

One negative consequence of harboring Feared Truths is that we don't embrace our positive qualities or personal strengths. For example, I often hear clients say that they can't take a compliment. In fact, they can barely hear or register compliments. Similarly, clients with Feared Truths often have difficulty thinking of positive attributes. It's as if they feel guilty about acknowledging the good because they're not acknowledging the bad, of which they're vaguely aware, but hiding. This is unfortunate because their good qualities are, in a sense, entirely separate from their Feared Truths. Hence, the "bad" shouldn't wash away the "good." Consequently, Feared Truths create a "double whammy": in with the bad and out with the good. Fortunately, once we accept our valid Feared Truths we become more capable of accepting our positive qualities as well, a healing outcome indeed!

Following the acceptance of decidedly valid Feared Truths, and the consequent development of healthier self-esteem, you don't allow *positive feedback* to influence your self-perception either. It's okay to feel good about someone's compliment, for example. But as the authority on your positive qualities, abilities, and performances, ask yourself whether or not that compliment is consistent with *your self-perception*. If it's not, readily acknowledge it as such, at least to yourself.

Having identified, explored, and accepted Feared Truths, you are in a better position to acknowledge positive self-attributes and feelings. I recommend that you generate a list of your positive qualities right now. Remember, these are qualities that *you decide* are accurate. Do your best to avoid picking positive qualities based on considerations of others' opinions of you. In addition, many people hesitate to list certain positive qualities because they can think of exceptions to them. I suggest that you include any positive qualities on your list that you think are generally true.

Begin generating your list of positive qualities by completing the three incomplete sentences below. Again, these sentences were borrowed from Nathaniel Branden's (1987) self-esteem work:

I like myself most when I—

It's easy for me to be self-accepting when I—

One of the things I like about myself best is—

You can expand on your list of positive qualities by considering your various roles in life. Are you a loving father, mother, grandmother, uncle, daughter, and so on? What are the qualities and behaviors which reflect being a good and loving so and so? Consider your "boy scout" qualities. Are you honest, fair, generous, loyal, and helpful? Are you a sensitive, caring, thoughtful, loving, and compassionate person? Are you structured, organized, disciplined, and hard working? What are your skills? Are you a good athlete, homemaker, student, teacher, painter, mechanic, boss, supervisor, seamstress, woodworker, or plumber?

Certain positive qualities are very meaningful because they express themselves in all contexts. One such quality is having good intentions, of meaning well. Even in the face of negative outcomes, if you trust that you meant well, you're unlikely to be as self-blaming, guilty, or doubtful.

Recall the experiences which suggest that you possess certain positive qualities. It's important that you evaluate the validity of your positive qualities by giving yourself a Fair Hearing in relation to these experiences. Enter the evidence potentially confirming or disconfirming these positives. Try to avoid others' opinions of your positive qualities. Judge for yourself, first and foremost, what *you* believe is true regarding these qualities. Discard the qualities that you don't accept as generally true. Allow yourself the time to embrace and feel good about the ones you do accept. Moreover, remind yourself of these positive qualities on a regular basis, in addition to the evidence supporting them.

6

The Difficulty of Accepting Feared Truths

Acceptance is a difficult concept because it's often equated with giving up, giving in, or surrender. Consequently, the idea of accepting Feared Truths may seem out of the question. Who would want to surrender to being dumb, ugly, a coward, and so on? "Won't this hurt too much?" "Won't I stagnate if I accept such a thing?" "Won't I get depressed?" These are good questions that clients often pose. We will respond to them shortly.

I define acceptance as acknowledging the factual basis of some quality of self. For instance, embrace *your* truth that your reading comprehension problem is a limitation, for example. In addition, acceptance reflects your willingness to feel the weight of a negative personal quality. It's important to accept something about yourself even if you don't like or feel good about it.

Acceptance, as reflected in a great deal of AA philosophy, is consistent with my use of the term. The rationale for a problem drinker to stand in front of his peers and admit, "I'm an alcoholic," is to prove his acceptance of the factual basis of this Feared Truth. Prior to such acceptance, his shame and embarrassment prompted him to hide his alcoholism from himself and others. He was more likely to continue drinking because he wasn't acknowledging the problem in the first place.

Another common phrase in AA circles is, "You're only as sick as your secrets." In other words, secrets lead to pretense, deceit, lies, betrayal, stagnation, and fears of exposure and rejection. Thus, the best path to change and recovery is to admit your secrets to yourself and others.

Why are my valid Feared Truths so difficult to accept? Why are they so scary? For one, I tend to see them as all or none. The idea that "I'm dumb" suggests I'm dumb, period, in everything. There is no qualifier here: I'm dumb. In addition, "I'm dumb" suggests that I'm nothing more. It's as if no other qualities exist or have relevance. "I'm dumb" is like saying, "I'm a bug," as if that describes me in my entirety.

The greater reality is that most of us are smart in some things and dumb in others, depending on how we define dumb. I *can* be dumb is probably more accurate. Most of us *can* be selfish, more or less. I *can* be bad-tempered, absent-minded, self-absorbed. In addition, "I'm dumb" (in some things) is one quality among many others.

Thus, Feared Truths often take the form of labels which characterize us in all or none fashion; they are generalizations. As a result, labels aren't the least bit fair or accurate because, by being so broad, they define us too narrowly. In addition, labels are typically communicated as if they're facts: Man, she's ugly!" In contrast to the overgeneralized and unqualified nature of labels, we rarely hear statements like, "*In my opinion*, I don't find you attractive, *although* I think you have nice teeth, pretty hair, and a nice complexion."

Feared Truths are difficult to accept because we equate them with inherent rejectability and inadequacy. Remember, children establish a sense of themselves through feedback. Growing up, many of us felt disliked, unloved, hated, or deficient, due to our so-called negative qualities or inadequacies. The implication was that we *had to be* handsome, smart, athletic, humble, selfless, honest, fair, giving, hardworking, loving, brave, and manly. We had to be *all* of these things. Then we felt safe. A flaw meant we were damaged goods. Such flaws became unacceptable because they made us dispensable, worthless, and unlovable. Worse, we adopted this mind-set in relationship to ourselves: "It mustn't be true that I'm that." We can't have flaws or imperfections and remain acceptable.

Thus, for many of us, our so-called childhood flaws became associated with painful, rejecting experiences. Adults criticized us angrily, even scornfully. Kids teased us mercilessly. In fact, our childhood peers can be the most painful sources of rejection. Children tend to be blunt, outspoken, concrete, and unqualified in what they say. They can be insensitive and have difficulty considering another person's vantage point. They are spontaneous and impulsive; they don't worry about saying the wrong thing at the wrong time. Comments like, "you're ugly," "your teeth are yucky," "your clothes have holes in them," "you have stupid sneakers," "your breath stinks," "I hate you," "you're not my friend," "nobody likes you," "he can't play, he's no good at anything," "you're always last," are typical. Children are literal in what they say and the recipients of such comments take them to heart. Such feedback really hurts. Being laughed at by kids causes a great deal of hurt, shame, and embarrassment too.

People who experienced more than their share of hurtful, childhood experiences fear more of the same as adults. Moreover, they can feel as vulnerable to rejection as did their childhood self.

Do you have to adhere to the formula, "flaws = rejection?" Can you be more accepting toward yourself regarding perceived, valid flaws? Marie couldn't. She feared that she was fat. I didn't try to convince her that she wasn't overweight. I tried to help her accept this belief, and to be willing to feel bad about it. She fought her belief about being overweight, rather than address her weight adaptively. This Feared Truth was so unacceptable that she fought a weight-war. She desperately battled her weight with laxatives, dehydration, vomiting, and so on. She was terrified, and her sense of urgency to eradicate her fat was overwhelming.

One variation on Feared Truths is to be *convinced* that a particular negative quality is true, while fearing the pain or shame associated with it. This is another reason why it can be so difficult to face a Feared Truth, one which, in this case, is more of a "Feared, Believed Truth."

For example, Claudette was born with an arm half the size of her "normal" arm. Throughout childhood she was made to feel as if it was grotesque, repulsive, and hideous. She was convinced that it made her extremely rejectable and inadequate. All of her life she tried to hide her arm to protect herself from further wounds. She hid from reminders of the past pain associated with it. By using it as little as possible, isolating, and never commenting on or drawing attention to it, she protected herself from anticipated pain. In the meantime, her arm was a constant source of shame and fear. She once told me that because of its functional necessity as a limb of her body, she had to live with its grotesqueness, implying that if it wasn't necessary, she'd have it amputated.

Because she was so convinced of its repulsiveness, I asked Claudette to list "what is right about my arm." This task was so novel she was bewildered in the face of it. While attempting this task, she frequently slipped into her negative beliefs about her arm.

Despite initial difficulty Claudette was able to list aspects of what was right about her arm. She acknowledged that its skin color was the same as the rest of her body, that it functioned adequately in particular ways, and that it looked exactly like her other arm except for its smaller size. These discoveries helped Claudette feel less hurt and afraid of how others might react to it.

Mindy didn't like her weight. She said that she wanted to lose one hundred pounds. Yet, she rarely mentioned this goal in therapy. I finally asked her how she felt about her weight. With some difficulty she said it made her feel "awful." Then she announced, "I don't want to feel awful about it!," as if trying to wish these feelings out of existence.

If Mindy went to her gym she imagined people would feel "awful" about her. Moreover, she'd feel awful about herself, a familiar feeling that she attempted to escape by avoiding the gym.

In essence, Mindy was imagining that others would feel toward her the way she felt about herself. Any evidence of their feelings would trigger her emotional awfulness, something she didn't want to experience. Therefore, she avoided the gym altogether.

Isn't it interesting that we imagine others will feel toward us the way we feel toward ourselves? Extending negative feelings about ourselves to others is a common psychological phenomenon. Consequently, we avoid what we feel and believe about ourselves by avoiding others, and by being impostors. Nevertheless, these strategies to escape from ourselves are no solution. We've simply compounded our trouble by implicating others in our feared-selves.

I suggested to Mindy that she embrace her awful feelings about her weight. In essence, she was avoiding and disowning feelings that were already present. It's as if she's holding an umbrella over her head in a thunder storm and pretending it's not raining because she's not getting wet. In addition, with a willingness to experience her feelings about her weight, she won't fear others with potentially critical reactions toward her. After all, she need not fear those who can trigger feelings which she's already been willing to feel.

The feeling of shame makes it extremely difficult to accept a Feared Truth. It's as if you're *inside* shame as you feel it. It's as if it's swallowing and suffocating you. Because it's a horrible feeling about yourself, and because you're drowning in it, you're desperate to escape it by any means. Yet, your shame can reflect your honest, emotional reactions *about* a decidedly valid Feared Truth. Thus, shame, as you reflect on it from the *outside*, often mirrors your values and self-ideal.

For many of us, shame means, "get that issue away from me." It means, "I'm so bad I can't stand it, get that reminder out of my sight." Shame is a reaction to yourself that you won't tolerate or accept. Yet, there it always is.

Experienced from the inside, shame is the feeling of hating yourself for what you are or for what you've done (or haven't done). It prompts you to run from the shame-inducing reality, thereby lessening your chances of change. From the outside, however, shame can be seen as a reflection of your values, morals, and ideals. It says, "I don't believe in what I did" and "I don't want to be the kind of person who does that." Your shame can work for you if it's seen in this light. By embracing the discomfort of shame with the recognition that it reflects your values and the person you aspire to become, it can motivate you to change. Furthermore, in your willingness to feel shame you can motivate yourself to change so you don't have to feel it again.

7

Accepting the Feelings of a Valid Feared Truth

Before confronting Feared Truths the feelings attached to them are buried. These feelings stir in their graves whenever you near them. Breaking ground, they rise. Terrified, you push them back down, giving them a sloppy reburial each time. At other times, it's no use, you can't push them away. You can't run fast or far enough. You're confronted with their identity and your worst, feared-self. Your personal nightmare, a feared version of yourself, is staring you in the face. Still, the feelings of fear, shame, guilt, pain, and self-loathing are temporary; you quickly exorcize them and your feared self back to the depths.

Before your courageous attempts to confront them, Feared Truths feel the most frightening. These vague enemies are hiding and lurking in the background of your awareness, ready to ambush you at any moment.

Identifying and exploring Feared Truths can't be worse than your lifetime of hiding from them, can they? Once identified, they're dealt with on your terms. Before, it was as if they had a life of their own, driving and influencing your behavior in painful, problematic ways seemingly beyond your control. But now, by identifying them, you begin to take control. By bringing them out of hiding and into the open they're finally exposed and have less power to dictate your behavior from behind the scenes. So go ahead, as slowly as you'd like, peek inside yourself, exposing the strangers within.

Upon discovering Feared Truths they're given faces or identities. The once unknown enemies become familiar and recognizable. As a result, they're not as scary. Later, when you learn about their histories and give them a Fair Hearing, you have a more emotionally balanced experience of them. Consistent with your Fair Hearing, perhaps you decide that some Feared Truths have no basis. On the other hand, you may decide that others are true and make sense, given your circumstances. Interestingly, if you decide that a Feared Truth is valid, your willingness to accept and tolerate its unpleasant feelings often helps with the acceptance of your positive qualities and feelings. In the past, harboring Feared Truths often left you feeling too guilty to accept your positive qualities. In turn, by embracing positive attributes and feelings, the negative feelings of your Feared Truth become balanced out, and hence, more tolerable.

Being your own judge, casting verdicts upon yourself, makes you stronger. Your ability and willingness to say, "I can be this and I don't like it," or "This is part of me, I wish it wasn't so, but it is," reflects a strength in you. It takes strength to lift the heavy burden of a Feared Truth, one which has been weighed down by painful, frightening feelings.

When you are willing to embrace a painful Feared Truth you're in a better position to reach out to it with compassion. You may be able to hug it tenderly as you would a wounded or scared child.

For example, given Claudette's negative attitude toward her smaller arm, I asked her to imagine sitting next to a child with the identical condition. Would she be as unkind and unloving toward that child as she's being toward herself? No. This experience helped Claudette feel more compassionate toward unwanted aspects of herself.

By exploring a Feared Truth with a Fair Hearing, its meaning and emotional tone changes. In his book, *Experiencing and the Creation of Meaning*, Eugene Gendlin (1962) says that "experiencing" is the always available, concretely present, flow of feeling. When you feel your body from the inside, with all of the thousands of different feeling tones and felt meanings, says Gendlin, you're in touch with that inner sense, that always available referent for your inward attention. At any given time you can always put a few aspects of the "felt-sense" of something into words. To Gendlin, the meaning of anything can always be located in your ever present and immediate experiencing or "felt-sense."

For example, we have all had the "felt-sense" of knowing we've forgotten something. We make some guesses and compare them against the "felt-sense" at hand, knowing when the guesses aren't right. They just don't feel right. When we recall the forgotten item we feel its rightness. The "felt- sense" of forgetting changes into one of remembering.

In any one moment I can focus attention on aspects of my felt experiencing. By staying with the feelings related to an issue, I can struggle to find words that seem to accurately describe its felt aspects. What first felt vague and confusing becomes clearer as I find the right words to describe feeling-based aspects of it. Finding the right words begins to change that issue's meaning as I bring it into clearer focus.

While writing a poem about winter, for example, I struggled to put into words the way the snow looked one moonlit night and how it made me feel. Yes, the snow was like a blanket, and the word, "blanket," captured a certain quality of the way it looked. It also captured some aspect of the coziness I felt. The word, "blanket," with its personal associations, interacted with the "felt-sense" of the experience I was trying to describe. A blend of meaning resulted while changing the "felt-sense" to something clear and experientially accurate.

This is what happens when you contact your "felt-sense" of a Feared Truth. At first, it's a vague, unformed, malformed, and biased Feared Truth because of how little it has been explored, described, and explained up until now. But as you look at, identify, and remember past experiences associated with it, it changes. The Feared Truth transforms as you give yourself a Fair Hearing about it. Its felt meaning changes with further elaboration. You see the Feared Truth in a newer, clearer light as you glean further perspective about it. In other words, your feelings in relation to a Feared Truth *have* to change as you describe, clarify, and explore the basis of it.

For example, for twenty years Sonny harbored and hid the fear that because he "allowed" a man on his paper route to molest him, he must have wanted it to happen, which is proof that he must be "gay." Associated with the memories of these molestation experiences were feelings of fear and shame sitting like a big rock in the pit of his stomach.

When Sonny finally acknowledged this Feared Truth and explored the experiences associated with it during a Fair Hearing, he remembered his boyish vulnerability to intense, adult manipulation. These detailed memories changed his fearful felt-sense that he "allowed" himself to be molested, as well as his grave concern that he must be "gay."

On the other hand, Sonny also remembered, quite unexpectedly, that he allowed his younger brother to take over his paper route without telling him or his parents about this child molester. He did so out of the sheer relief of his own escape. Nevertheless, Sonny choose to embrace deep shame for not protecting his brother from a similar fate. Accepting such shame, or for that matter, any unpleasant feeling associated with a valid Feared Truth, takes a great deal of courage. Despite the price of feeling the weight of such a feeling, Sonny experienced tremendous relief from the self-protective, escapist strategies of hiding this Feared Truth from himself and others.

8

Accepting Valid Feared Truths without Trying to Change Them

WHAT SHOULD YOU DO with decidedly valid Feared Truths? Your task is to accept the factual basis of their existence, along with how they make you feel. It must sound awfully callous of me to ask you to accept the belief and feelings about some despised personal quality that you've hidden for much of your life. But, as a necessary first step toward possible change, this may be your best solution.

You may ask, what if there is no escape from, for example, being unattractive? What then?

What is gained? First of all, by owning the decided, factual basis of a Feared Truth, along with your feelings about it, you won't be as vulnerable to other people. They can no longer shock or overwhelm you with negative feedback about your appearance because you are no longer hiding from the basis of such feedback; you're already super-familiar with the issue and its personal and emotional significance. Furthermore, that feedback isn't as frightening in its potential to hurt because you *already feel hurt about it*. In your willingness to embrace *your* pain, no one can make you feel worse about it than you already do. In general, you are knowing yourself better than anyone else can. You've become the ultimate authority on you, the one with the last say or final verdict, the superior court judge over-ruling all other circuit court judges.

Another gain from accepting a Feared Truth, rather than despising, hating, and running from it, is that you are standing with yourself, as if saying, "We're in this together." Instead of ignoring, hiding from, and rejecting your feared-self, you are expressing an attitude of loyalty and partnership toward it.

It is normal to want to change a Feared Truth into something about which you can feel proud. But when you decide to face a Feared Truth, your primary motive can't be that of changing it as fast as possible just to get rid of it. Initially, your motive must reflect a willingness to grasp the truth of an attribute you've been hiding from. Hold it tight, as if it is trying to run away from you! Allow it to exist out in the open, right in front of you. Get to know it better while feeling all of its impact.

You can't let something go until you embrace it. Therefore, if your motive from the start is to escape a Feared Truth, the genuineness of your Fair Hearing will be tainted, as if you had tampered with a jury. If your primary motive for facing a Feared Truth is one of ultimate escape from it, your Fair Hearing will likely be superficial, vague, and biased in the direction of passing a not-guilty verdict; you will deem the Feared Truth has having no validity. As a result, you may have broken the stem, but the roots of the

Feared Truth will still be there, resurfacing at some later time in familiar, problematic fashion.

Once you have completed the hard work of fully facing, embracing, and accepting a valid Feared Truth, along with the unpleasant feelings associated with it, then it's safe to decide if it is something you can change. Many clients of mine have embraced and accepted decidedly valid, emotionally unpleasant Feared Truths: Jim hired a tutor and learned how to read; Beth had her over-bite corrected; Cheryl lost sixty pounds; Sarah explored her sexual preference; Sue finally left her alcoholic husband; Al learned Karate to overcome his sense of cowardice. Much to their surprise, they found it easier to change a Feared Truth because they weren't trying to escape it out of desperation, fear, and urgency.

Perhaps you too can change a decidedly valid Feared Truth once you have accepted it as a personal fact, along with its unpleasant feelings. If you think you can, go for it! Because you are more familiar and acquainted with the unpleasant feelings attached to the Feared Truth, your motive may be less one of escape, and more one of pride as you courageously face and explore it. Less desperate, afraid, and urgent, you may be able to stay the course of change in a more organized and disciplined fashion. As a result, your chances of success are greater.

9

Investment in Feared Truths

Accepting valid Feared Truths is very difficult, but discarding *invalid* ones can be even more challenging. Why would it be difficult to accept that a feared personal quality has no basis, especially when a Fair Hearing resulted in the verdict of not-guilty? It may be a huge shock, but many people are invested in holding onto invalid negative qualities without even knowing it!

Leanne had such an investment. She grew up being physically and emotionally abused by her mother. As an adult, Leanne chastised herself over the same things her mom berated. She also blamed herself for the fact that her mom abused her. When she attempted a Fair Hearing about her Feared Truths, she seemed to stubbornly resist doing so. Guessing that she might be invested in harboring Feared Truths, I asked Leanne to close her eyes and imagine seeing herself in a positive light, and hence, not blaming herself for being abused. Upon opening her eyes she said that if she saw herself in a positive light it would prove that her mother had been wrong about her. In turn, Leanne would be filled with rage. As the target of this rage, her mom might reject Leanne. This rejection would ruin her fantasy of having a caring, nurturing mother.

Despite the price Leanne paid for seeing herself in a negative light and blaming herself over being abused, it somehow (unconsciously) seemed a lesser price to pay than that of alienating her mom. Angrily blaming her mother might sacrifice any chance of having the loving parent she always wanted.

Bruce Ecker and Laurel Hulley (1996) are psychotherapists who construe the human psyche as extremely clever and adaptive: symptoms don't exist randomly or without purpose. The psyche is presented with the amazingly difficult task of juggling and balancing a variety of contradictory needs, feelings, and desires, across various roles, contexts, and experiences (past, present, and future). Ecker and Hulley believe that the psyche utilizes a particular symptom, which is consciously unwanted and unpleasant, to protect oneself from some other unwanted outcome. Freud (1961) realized this as well. He believed that the human psyche sought compromises among its different aspects (ego, id, and superego) to achieve a balance of their disparate needs, values, goals, and ways of functioning.

For instance, Russ is chronically anxious and insecure about performing well and living up to expectations. One day, while talking to Russ about a golf tournament, he mentioned playing well, but quickly changed topics. Later, I asked him how he did and much to my surprise he said he won the tournament! We explored similar instances, such as minimizing his neighbor's compliments about how well he landscaped his yard.

I asked Russ to imagine acknowledging his strengths and abilities in various situations where he hadn't done so in the past. He imagined that people would be rejecting for making them feel insecure in the light of his strengths. He recalled that his father couldn't tolerate young Russ' successes or proud feelings; his father became angry, critical, and rejecting in response. Russ learned that it was safer to disavow any positive abilities, successes, or feelings of pride. Again, he preferred the price he paid for never letting himself feel good about his successes (albeit, unconsciously), rather than risk anticipated angry rejection.

If you are having trouble discarding what you recognize as an invalid Feared Truth, consider the *negative* consequences which might arise as you imagine *no longer having it*. Remember a specific situation when you struggled with that Feared Truth. Close your eyes and *imagine* yourself in that situation *without* the Feared Truth. Consider the negative consequences which could arise during that situation as a result of its absence. This can help you understand motives of which you were unaware and which support your potential need to have the Feared Truth.

After identifying one or more protective motives for holding onto a Feared Truth, ask yourself if it's worth the price you pay for doing so. You may genuinely decide that it's worth it. If so, continue on as you have. However, if you decide that the price is too high, let go of the Feared Truth. But be prepared for negative consequences that the Feared Truth protected you from.

You can utilize Nathaniel Branden's (1987) incomplete sentences to identify motives of which you may be unaware, and which keep you invested in holding onto invalid Feared Truths. Many of these sentences help you identify the potential negative consequences of feeling good about yourself. Therefore, if the sentence endings are filled with negative consequences, you are probably invested in seeing yourself in a negative light, and therefore, in holding onto Feared Truths.

If I were to admit the things I feel pride about—

The scary thing about being self-accepting is—

If I were more accepting of my body—

If I were more accepting of the things I have done—

If I were more accepting of my feelings—

If I were to admit how much I secretly like myself—

If it turns out I'm not a bad person and never was—

The good thing about pretending to dislike myself is—

If I had the courage to admit that whatever my shortcomings, I like myself—

If I were to accept ______ completely—
(fill in the blank with each of your Feared Truths)

The scary thing about admitting pride in myself or my accomplishments is—

Let's look at another instance of investment in an invalid Feared Truth. Sasha was talking about how a new man in her life was treating her. She couldn't believe he was so caring and attentive. She was afraid it would come to an end. Her tone implied that she couldn't believe that someone could possibly love her enough to treat her so well.

In contrast, Sasha's relationship with her inattentive husband, Fred, was coming to an end after twenty years of marriage. She didn't feel valued by Fred, whereas Earl's love was a dream come true. Fred knew Sasha had essentially chosen Earl so he decided to leave the family home. His departure left Sasha with tremendous guilt.

While Sasha discussed her fear of losing Earl's love, she mentioned feeling "deserted" by Fred. I quickly reminded her that Fred didn't desert her; he made the only choice he could, given her decision to be with Earl. I also reminded Sasha of a prior session when I asked her to consider whether or not therapy was helping her, a question which prompted tears on her part. Surprised, I asked her what was wrong and she said that I was dumping her just like everyone else. We spent the remainder of the hour clarifying this matter.

Sasha had clearly distorted my question into a rejecting message. Similarly, she distorted Fred's role in ending their marriage. In each case, she was seeing herself as the victim of rejection.

In essence, she was saying, "I'm totally rejectable." I told her that she seemed motivated to see herself as rejectable and unlovable, as evidenced by distortions of the facts at hand.

Given this apparent motivation I asked Sasha to imagine leaving my office, miraculously thinking of herself in primarily positive terms. In other words, I asked her to imagine herself without the Feared Truth of being inherently rejectable. I asked her to imagine that Earl was lucky to have her. What negative consequences might result from these imagined scenarios? She answered, "If I felt good about myself and Earl rejected me, I'd feel horrible. I'd feel far worse than if I had felt bad about myself and he rejected me." Thus, Sasha lessens the emotional fall of rejection if she already feels unworthy.

Sasha and I agreed that she's motivated to perceive herself as rejectable to protect herself from tremendous pain, should rejection occur. She realized that the price she pays for this protection is too high. She takes few risks getting close to others. She becomes the person she feels she is: "By seeing myself as ugly, I don't fix my hair or try to look pretty, and I actually become ugly." She then gets depressed. Therefore, she decided to notice any self-berating thoughts or expectations of rejection, to remind herself of their protective function, to challenge their legitimacy, and to acknowledge her positive qualities.

10

Living Feared Truths

PUNISH ME

ELAINE, a divorced mother of two girls, came to therapy reporting a lifetime of depressive feelings, low self-esteem, social anxiety and avoidance, fears of conflict, and difficulty setting limits and being assertive. In her first session we explored some difficult interactions she had with co-workers. We realized that she felt guilty and feared being punished during interactions which were confrontational. Even in situations where it was certain she did nothing wrong, she felt guilty. Moreover, she seemed invested in proving she had done something wrong when she clearly hadn't.

I worked with Elaine two years earlier and knew about her childhood history of sexual abuse. However, the crisis of her divorce dominated our sessions at that time. At the end of our first session upon her return to therapy I wondered aloud if her guilt, fear, and depression might be related to her history of abuse. We agreed to explore that history during our next session.

Growing up, Elaine had four brothers, two of whom were older and abused her sexually. Yet, she did not seem as traumatized by this fact as she was by having initiated sexual contact with her two younger brothers. She cried as she contacted her feelings of guilt and shame about Dennis and Lane. She said that she felt "awful," "bad," and "to blame." She finally identified her Feared Truth that she was a sexual abuser.

To explore this Feared Truth, Elaine recalled her subjective experience during these traumatic childhood events. The adult Elaine, accustomed to being out of touch with the details of her childhood, often intruded into this process of recollection, guilt-ridden and terrified of staying close to her subjective experience. Nevertheless, she recalled her "impoverished" home life at that time. Her parents expressed little love, affection, or attention. She generally felt sad and lonely. She recalled feelings of powerlessness and helplessness at the hands of her older brothers. In contrast, she felt in control and powerful when initiating sexual contact with her younger brothers. Something about this power felt important to her: it was a welcome departure from her usual feelings of vulnerability. She also recalled that the contact with her younger brothers felt nice. She remembered that her contact with Lane was mutual. However, on the first occasion of inappropriately touching Dennis, she immediately stopped when she sensed his discomfort. It reminded her of the discomfort she felt at the hands of her older brothers: "I didn't want to do that to Dennis."

These recollections helped Elaine. They weren't excuses to talk herself out of her responsibility for what happened. They were, to her, accurate descriptions of what she remembered. As such, they brought a new perspective, helping her treat and judge herself less harshly. She refused to relinquish all of her responsibility in what happened, holding onto some guilt and shame about her role in it. She even came to view these feelings as proof that she has a conscience and is basically a good person.

As a test of whether or not she had accepted her Feared Truth and its accompanying feelings, I asked Elaine to tell a friend about what happened in her childhood. She never told anyone about this but me. We role-played this potential encounter. She felt and believed herself to be okay even as I criticized her. Elaine said that by allowing herself to feel bad about her role with Lane, with a clear view of the evidence which confirmed and disconfirmed her culpability in it, my pretend criticism was manageable. For the first time in her life Elaine felt as if she could own her guilty feelings safely.

One month later, during our last session together, Elaine reported that she told a friend about her child abuse history. She added that she felt totally different about herself. She felt as if walls had dropped from all around her. She discovered that she could clearly hear others who talked to her, as if for the first time. She felt less anxious and scared of confrontations. She was better at setting limits with her children and others. She no longer felt automatically guilty and at fault in situations of conflict.

Elaine's work highlights a number of important facets on which we've touched. Because she was courageous enough to explore her subjective past, she touched on the evidence both confirming and disconfirming her Feared Truth. As a result of this Fair Hearing, she gleaned a more balanced and accurate perspective about her feared role at that time. She still felt guilty about her behavior with her younger brothers and was willing to embrace it. She was accepting her decidedly valid sense of responsibility, along with her feelings about it. Even when I criticized her during our role-playing she held firm to her own evidence, experience, and opinions. She finally told her friend about her past, confident that she need not be rescued from her fears nor protected from potential negative reactions.

SPELLING BEE SCARED

Laurel was a sixty year old woman who came to therapy feeling very depressed because of her work in the mail-room of her company. In fact, she was so depressed that she took a medical leave of absence. Laurel was once offered a chance to run the mail-room but she turned it down because she was afraid of misspelling words in a mail-room manager's log book. She was frightened of feeling humiliated if others discovered her spelling errors. Consequently, she found herself being supervised by a very young woman named Susan, whom she initially admired. Laurel also envied Susan because she was pretty, smart, and had a great deal of potential.

Over the course of their work together Laurel became extremely upset to see Susan wasting her potential, potential she sensed within herself but failed to realize. But most of all, Susan made Laurel feel "small, insecure, less than, and stupid." Laurel's depression stemmed from these feelings. She was unable to assert herself with Susan, as a result. Consequently, she felt increasingly "walked on" by Susan and had to leave work because she was extremely depressed.

Laurel recalled that when she was in grade school she couldn't spell. She did poorly in the frequent spelling bees of her class and remembers being humiliated by her teacher and fellow students. In addition, her father would drill her every evening in spelling. He frequently became frustrated and angry with her inability to do it well.

These grade school and home experiences left Laurel certain that she was dumb. She spent the remainder of her school years avoiding difficult classes and focusing on a home economics curriculum. She longed for something more academically challenging but feared she lacked the potential to succeed.

Laurel and I talked about her spelling problem and agreed that she probably had a learning disability. We also agreed that, in those days, they didn't know about learning disabilities. Consequently, she was labeled and treated as if she was dumb.

Laurel couldn't remain angry at her teachers given her new understanding of their ignorance about learning disabilities. In addition, she talked to a neighbor who taught learning disabled children to better understand the nature of her difficulty. Although she felt bad about herself for having this deficit, she felt worse when she feared being dumb.

Laurel realized that her fear of being dumb had stopped her from being smart. It stopped her from taking risks that would have helped her feel smart. Thus, instead of being dumb, she started to see herself as having been *afraid* of being dumb. She also decided that she's quite smart in a number of ways.

Instead of seeing herself as dumb Laurel decided that she had a learning disability. As therapy came to a close she believed that she could be open about this fact if need be. She also decided to pursue some academic challenges, ones she'd avoided out of fear of being exposed as dumb.

Lastly, Laurel decided that she would only return to work if she were placed in the supervisory position in the mail-room. This was the first time she discussed returning to work without feeling afraid of doing so. Ultimately, however, Laurel decided not to return to work at all. She'd worked hard all of her life, carrying the constant burden of being exposed as dumb, so she decided that she deserved to retire.

THE SOPHISTICATED CHARMING SLUT

When Lucy was a girl she felt hurt and disappointed by her mother. To make matters worse, her mom seemed to love her brothers more, and was very interested in helping others. Convinced that something must be wrong with her, Lucy worked extra hard to win her mother's approval. She became her mother's comforter, entertainer, and rescuer. But no matter what she did her mom remained disinterested in her. Consequently, Lucy came to hate her mom because she was convinced that her mother didn't love her.

Lucy said she developed low self-esteem as a child. The kids at school and from her neighborhood made her feel like a "scrawny, loud, obnoxious, ugly, welfare case." As she moved into early adolescence, she came to see herself as an even uglier, acne-riddled girl. She eventually added liar, fake, and slut to her self-perception.

When Lucy turned eighteen years of age she had a body toward which men seemed attracted. For the first time ever somebody seemed interested in her. She began to wear more provocative clothes and relished the extra attention men gave her. In addition, she discovered that using drugs and alcohol brought her greater acceptance among her new friends. Over time, however, she had a number of traumatic experiences with men. These experiences left her feeling used, dirty, and sluttish.

When I met Lucy she was a forty-one-year-old wife and mother. After seventeen years of raising children she longed for the partying, excitement, and attention she once enjoyed from men. She became increasingly immersed in such activities, creating a series of crises for herself and her family.

A number of themes became clear during our therapeutic work. For one, Lucy feared making commitments to people outside her immediate family. She said that she couldn't trust herself to "come through" for others. She said that she would inevitably hurt and disappoint them. She feared their rejection and the anticipated horrible feelings about herself. She further imagined that they would hate her and believe she didn't care about them. We realized that she imagined others would feel toward her what she felt toward her mom as a young girl. This possibility really frightened her.

When we met, Lucy was heavier than she'd ever been in her life. She became extremely angry at her husband, Bob, when he voiced health concerns about her weight. She didn't believe he was actually concerned about her health. Instead, she believed that Bob, like every man, was only interested in her if she was thin and pretty or "put out" sexually. If a man doesn't think she's attractive, she thought, he can't love her. Therefore, she has to rely on sex to keep him interested. Believing herself to be unattractive and sexually easy made her feel "used, unwanted, unattractive, dirty, cheap, disrespected, and sluttish."

Lucy and I realized that she was using her body and sexuality to get the attention and affection of men in the same way she did as an eighteen-year-old. She frequented bars and nightclubs, flirting with men at every turn. Yet, she was conflicted: she wanted men to be attracted to, lust for, and desire her, but feared men over sexualizing her. She tried to strike a balance between her desire and fear by presenting herself as a "whole sexual package." She dressed and acted in a way which she hoped would be seen as "sophisticated, charming, intelligent, discreet, and subtly sexual."

One evening, Lucy enjoyed talking with a man whom she thought really liked her. At the end of the night he indicated that he wanted to have sex. His sexual desire left her feeling like "all the rest of it wasn't real," meaning, he couldn't have really liked or have been attracted to her. His desire for sex "ruined" it. This episode reconfirmed that, "All men want is sex, not me, not who I am."

Despite her greater understanding of her needs, insecurities, and behavioral tendencies, Lucy couldn't stop chasing the party life and the desire to flirt with men. We discussed the origins of this apparent need. She recognized that her behavior was connected to childhood insecurities and to her attractiveness to men as a young woman. To help further explore her insecurities, I asked Lucy to imagine herself at a party. What would hurt the most if she could eavesdrop on conversations about her afterwards? After a minute of silence she said that she feared being seen as scrawny, loud, obnoxious, ugly, as having a big nose, bad hair, and for being a liar, fake, slut, and welfare case. We immediately recognized these as self and other-perceptions she experienced as a child and adolescent. These were Lucy's Feared Truths, despite the fact that such physical qualities no longer existed.

Lucy's two biggest Feared Truths concerned being unattractive and slutty. Feeling unattractive stemmed from feedback regarding her appearance as a child and adolescent. To disconfirm and compensate for this fear of being unattractive she used sex to gain the interest of men. But these sexual experiences left her fearing that she was a slut.

Lucy and I explored her sexual history with men as a way to give her a Fair Hearing about being a slut. Lucy recalled having sex with Brian, a man to whom she should have said "no." This left her feeling dirty, used, and slutty. We looked closely at the reasons why she didn't say "no." She recalled that shortly before sex with Brian her father called her a slut. She angrily stormed out of the house wanting to make it true as a way to lash out at him. She also recalled wanting to be liked, and to remain part of Brian's social circle. She feared that resisting sex would lead to alienation from him and his friends. She also remembered being jealous of her sister, toward whom Brian was attracted. She thought that she could keep Brian and hurt her sister if she had sex with him. Furthermore, because Brian controlled everything, and acted as if he owned her, it was difficult for her to set limits. Lastly, Lucy remembered that by the time she really wanted to say "no," it was too late. She'd gone too far to turn back without being angrily blamed for being a "tease."

There were many experiences which left Lucy fearing she was a slut, but as you can see from this one, she had many reasons for having sex and not saying "no." It became clear to her, in this case, that she didn't have sex because she was a slut. She felt incredibly relieved as a result.

Tragically, Lucy has spent all of her life trying to disconfirm her Feared Truths. She's attempted to disconfirm her Feared Truth of being unattractive by being sexually appealing to men. Unfortunately, this created the new Feared Truth of being a slut. She's tried to disconfirm her Feared Truth of being a slut by behaving in a sophisticated, charming, discreet, and subtly sexual fashion. Unfortunately, this behavior inevitably led to sex, which reinforced her fears of being a slut. She tried to disconfirm her Feared Truth of being a disappointment to others by avoiding any commitments to them, but this too created the very outcome she was trying to avoid.

The consequences of Lucy's strategies to disconfirm her Feared Truths have been devastating. Obviously, she needed to find a new way of coping with them. She identified her Feared Truths and was gleaning an understanding of the negative consequences of her disconfirming strategies. She also started the process of courageously exploring her sexual history to give herself a Fair Hearing about her Feared Truth of being a slut.

During our last therapy session I asked Lucy to consider the negative consequences if men no longer saw her as sexually appealing. She said she'd feel "empty, a void, useless, and like nothing." The idea of losing this source of self-esteem was terrifying. Lacking this coping strategy would leave her face-to-face with the fear of her unattractiveness and she just couldn't risk it. This risk frightened her so much that she dropped out of therapy.

THE MOST BEAUTIFUL WOMAN OF ALL

Mary came to therapy fretting about her eye condition, one which developed after lying in a tanning bed for too long without eye protection. She consistently berates herself for ignoring her concerns of potentially harming herself in the booth. Interestingly, she ignored her concerns because she feared damage to herself already, and the anticipated harshness toward herself in response.

A week after our first meeting Mary became concerned about hearing loss suffered while listening to her "boom box" for too long. Again, she ignored initial concerns about damaging her hearing because she feared damage already and didn't want to admit it. She feared yet another deficiency and further self-blaming.

During our first two sessions Mary indicated that she can't tolerate deficiencies. She said that she had to feel as if she were "the most beautiful of all." She had to be smart too; if she wasn't "quick enough" with answers to questions, she had to make up excuses to explain why. She added that she obsessed about a little scar on her nose which developed after picking at a pimple for too long. Once, upon asking her to characterize her appearance, she balked on exploring her perceptions of her breasts: "What if I decide I don't like them?!"

When I asked Mary about why deficiencies are so unacceptable, she said that her father often exclaimed, "We're Martins!" This meant that they were better than other people. He was a "strong attorney," admired among his family and friends. He continually preached about the importance of strength and independence.

During our third session Mary said that her hearing was improving and that someone had told her it would heal over time. "Nature takes care of itself" and "Time heals all wounds," she confidently stated. However, she added that she'd taken too much niacin in an attempt to correct her hearing loss. Consequently, she broke out in a skin rash which she attributed to an overdose of the vitamin.

Mary once told me that there was nothing about oneself that couldn't be changed. She believed that anything could be corrected and turned into something positive, a strength or asset. She added that she hated the "Serenity Prayer" because it advocates accepting things you cannot change: "There's nothing you can't change." Mary said that as a child she was told that flaws were her fault because any deficiency could be corrected if she tried hard enough. Thus, the presence of one flaw is indicative of the presence of another: you're too lazy to overcome it. This belief prompted her to do something about her hearing loss rather than letting nature take its course.

I asked Mary to imagine being in a car accident and losing a leg. However, I wave my magic wand and she can't think of any way of undoing this reality. What would this be like for her? Mary said, "I'd feel hopeless and self-blaming, and I'd have thoughts like, 'If I hadn't done such and such,' and 'If only's,' and 'How could I have's.' I'd feel depressed, panicky, and afraid, like an emergency. I'd give myself pep talks, 'Life's still worth it,' to try to switch off these feelings, but it wouldn't last. I'd feel deficient, less a person, lacking ... not up to standard, the definition of a failure, and like something's wrong with me."

I then asked Mary, "What's the significance of this deficiency of having no leg?" She said, "Like the world is too difficult ... it was already hard enough when everything was working ... I can't handle it. I don't want to deal with it ... I can't be that strong, don't make me be that strong, it's asking too much to be a stronger person ... don't make me do that, it's too hard. Part of me wants to be weak and dependent but I'm supposed to be strong."

I told Mary that deficiencies or flaws seemed unacceptable because they reflect weakness and dependency, qualities which are even more unacceptable. She said, "Underneath it all I feel I'm not strong, I'm weak, my mother thought I was weak as a child, and still does. She would say, 'You're not a strong person' and 'You shouldn't work anyway.' My father's family viewed my mom negatively. They saw her as weak, as unable to cope due to her nervous breakdowns. My father's relatives would whisper about me, 'She's just like her mother,' thinking I couldn't hear, but I could." Thus, growing up, there were strongly stated injunctions against being weak and dependent, and equally strong expectations to be a Martin, strong and independent.

I asked Mary if part of her *wanted* to be weak and dependent. What might be nice about it? She said, "It was nice with mom. Even two weeks ago, mom said, 'Why don't you come here? I'll take care of you, you're not strong, you need to rest.' I said, 'Maybe I'll stay two or three days.' She said, 'You can stay as long as you like.' She meant that she wanted me to stay for months. 'You're my daughter, I'll always be here for you, let me take care of you.' It was kind of tempting. But if I do that I'm going to have to come back to reality. I also want to have kids, to be a mom, and be involved in a relationship with a man, and that would take me from that part of life, and the time clock is ticking."

Mary's problems were clearer to both of us. She experienced a long-standing inability to tolerate any self-perceived deficiencies or flaws, utilizing a number of strategies to deny, ignore, change, and disconfirm such Feared Truths. Deficiencies were seen as harbingers of her Feared Truth of unacceptable weakness and dependency, the opposite of being a strong and independent Martin.

Mary began questioning her now conscious premise that weakness and dependency are inherently unacceptable and rejectable qualities which preclude strength and independence. Maybe there are grey areas here, ones that can vary daily? Maybe she need not fear her flaws so much? "Just thinking I'd be worthwhile even if I have flaws is difficult to accept," she said with great seriousness and thoughtfulness. She considered accepting the flaws she believes are true, as well as her feelings about them, without believing that they make her absolutely weak and dependent.

A year or two after our initial work together Mary had a miscarriage which she genuinely believed was her fault. Amazingly, she accepted this reality without harshly criticizing herself. She was finally accepting the valid Feared Truth of her imperfection as a human being.

These four therapy clients spent their adult lives trying to avoid Feared Truths. They were trying to protect their sense of self from further harm. But by attempting to hide Feared Truths from themselves and others, they experienced a myriad of unpleasant symptoms. In addition, they were impostors to themselves and others, carrying the huge burden of protecting their shadow-selves from being discovered and exposed to the world. Finally, their suffering became too much to bear and they mustered the courage to face their frightening secret-selves.

As a first step, these clients faced and identified their Feared Truths. Then they allowed themselves to be their own defense attorney, prosecuting attorney, judge, and jury. In essence, they put their Feared Truths on trial in an attempt to give themselves a Fair Hearing. Still more bravery was required if the verdict passed was guilty as charged. Their willingness to own a flaw, negative quality, or regretted action, along with its associated feelings, and to potentially acknowledge it to the world, represented their final acts of bravery. Paradoxically, in so doing, they experienced tremendous freedom by releasing themselves from the holding cell of low self-esteem to which they also held guard.

If you are like me or ninety percent of the high functioning people I see in therapy, you've been caught in a habit left over from childhood: looking to and depending on others to feel good about yourself. As a child inherently vulnerable to negative feedback you've been contaminated with certain feared beliefs about yourself, ones associated with feelings of rejection and inadequacy. These Feared Truths have been so scary and painful that, until now, you've hidden them from yourself, sensing their potential truth, but not wanting to find out for sure. Even worse, every day of your adult life you've tried to ensure that these feared personal qualities were never exposed to others; you haven't wanted to confront their potential truth and supposed rejection-prompting nature. So you've been an impostor to yourself and others, paying the price of social anxiety and other unpleasant emotions and outcomes, at least, until now. By reading this book, I hope that you feel significant relief from having faced, perhaps, your worst fears (about yourself). If you took the next step and genuinely explored their personal validity through the Fair Hearing process, then you're on the path of being the authority of who you are. Practice being that self-authority by coming back to what you know about yourself in the face of negative and positive feedback, and relish the priceless freedom of no longer having your self-perception determined by others. Wahoo!

Bibliography

Adler, A. (1929). *The Practice and Theory of Individual Psychotherapy*. New York: Harcourt Brace Jovanovich.

Berne, E. (1974). *What Do You Say After You Say Hello?* New York: Banton.

Bishop, J. & Grunte, M. (1992). *How to Love Yourself When You Don't Know How*. Barrytown, N.Y.: Station Hill Press.

Bradshaw, J. E. (1988). *Healing the Shame That Binds You*. Deerfield Beech, Florida: Health-Communications, Inc.

Bradshaw, J. E. (1990). *Home Coming: Reclaiming and Championing Your Inner Child*. New York: Bantam Books.

Branden, N. (1971). *The Psychology of Self-Esteem*. New York: Bantam Books.

Branden, N. (1972). *Breaking Free*. New York: Bantam Books.

Branden, N. (1985). *Honoring the Self: Self-Esteem and Personal Transformation*. New York: Bantam Books.

Branden, N. (1987). *How to Raise Your Self-Esteem*. Toronto; New York: Bantam Books.

Branden, N. (1994). *The Six Pillars of Self-Esteem.* New York: Bantam Books.

Ecker, B. and Hulley, L. (1996). *Depth Oriented Brief Therapy: How to Be Brief When You Were Trained to Be Deep and Vice Versa*. San Francisco: Jossey-Bass.

Freud, S. (1961). *The Standard Edition of the Complete Psychological Works of Sigmund Freud*. 24 volumes, translated and edited by James Strachey. London: Hogarth Press and the Institute of Psychoanalysis.

Gendlin, E. (1962). *Experiencing and the Creation of Meaning*. New York: Free Press.

Jung, C. G. (1950). *The Collected Works of C.G. Jung*. Adler G., Fordham, M. and Reed, H., eds.; Hall, R.F.C., trans. Bolliger Series XX, Princeton: Princeton University Press.

McGinnis, A. L. (1987). *Confidence: How to Succeed at Being Yourself.* Minneapolis: Augsburg Publishing House.

Newman, M. & Berkowitz, B. (1971). *How to Be Your Own Best Friend.* New York: Random House.

Wilber, K. (1996). *The Atman Project: A Transpersonal View of Human Development*. Wheaton: Quest Books.

About the Author

Herbert S. Demmin received his Ph.D. in Clinical Psychology from Texas Tech University in 1986. He has worked as a Staff Clinical Psychologist for the Department of Veterans Affairs in Livermore, California, and Brookside Hospital in New Hampshire. He presently has a private group practice in Nashua, NH. He is the co-author of the "Psychodynamic Psychotherapy" section of an *Introduction to Clinical Psychology* text book. He is also having a life-work published in 2003, titled *The Ghosts of Consciousness: Understanding Thought and the Illusory Self on the Spiritual Path*. Dr. Demmin is an expert on the treatment of low self-esteem and on the nature of thinking. He and his loving daughter, Veronica, currently live in Nashua, NH.

Printed in the United States
840500001B